EATING RIGHT WITH MYPLATE

Protein Foods Group

by Megan Borgert-Spaniol

BLASTOFF!
2
READERS

BELLWETHER MEDIA · MINNEAPOLIS, MN

Note to Librarians, Teachers, and Parents:

Blastoff! Readers are carefully developed by literacy experts and combine standards-based content with developmentally appropriate text.

Level 1 provides the most support through repetition of high-frequency words, light text, predictable sentence patterns, and strong visual support.

Level 2 offers early readers a bit more challenge through varied simple sentences, increased text load, and less repetition of high-frequency words.

Level 3 advances early-fluent readers toward fluency through increased text and concept load, less reliance on visuals, longer sentences, and more literary language.

Level 4 builds reading stamina by providing more text per page, increased use of punctuation, greater variation in sentence patterns, and increasingly challenging vocabulary.

Level 5 encourages children to move from "learning to read" to "reading to learn" by providing even more text, varied writing styles, and less familiar topics.

Whichever book is right for your reader, Blastoff! Readers are the perfect books to build confidence and encourage a love of reading that will last a lifetime!

This edition first published in 2012 by Bellwether Media, Inc.

No part of this publication may be reproduced in whole or in part without written permission of the publisher. For information regarding permission, write to Bellwether Media, Inc., Attention: Permissions Department, 5357 Penn Avenue South, Minneapolis, MN 55419.

Library of Congress Cataloging-in-Publication Data

Borgert-Spaniol, Megan, 1989-
  Protein foods group / by Megan Borgert-Spaniol.
    p. cm. – (Blastoff! readers. Eating right with myplate)
  Summary: "Relevant images match informative text in this introduction to the protein foods group. Intended for students in kindergarten through third grade"– Provided by publisher.
  Includes bibliographical references and index.
  ISBN 978-1-60014-759-3 (hardcover : alk. paper)
  1. Proteins in human nutrition–Juvenile literature. I. Title.
TX553.P7B67 2012
613.2′82–dc23   2011033125

Printed in the United States of America, North Mankato, MN.
010112   1207

Contents

The Protein Foods Group

The Protein Foods Group includes meat, **poultry**, fish, and eggs.

Beans, nuts, and seeds also
belong to the group.

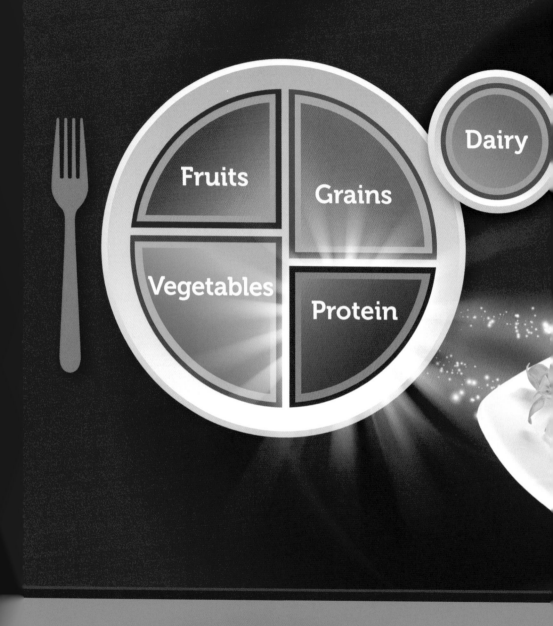

The Protein Foods Group is the purple part of **MyPlate**.

1 serving = 1 egg
1 tablespoon peanut butter
2 tablespoons hummus
½ bean burger patty
½ small lean hamburger
1 slice turkey

Kids need four servings of protein foods each day.

Why Are Protein Foods Good For You?

Protein foods provide your body with **amino acids**.

Amino acids are the building blocks of bones, muscles, skin, and blood.

Protein foods also have **iron** and **B vitamins**. These give you energy to run and play.

Some fish and nuts are rich in **omega-3**. This is good for your heart.

Choosing Protein Foods

Choose **lean** meats and skinless poultry. They have less **fat**.

Some meats have added **sodium**. Find meats that are low in sodium.

Eat nuts or seeds with
some meals.

Choose unsalted nuts and
seeds. They are low in sodium.

Eating Protein Foods

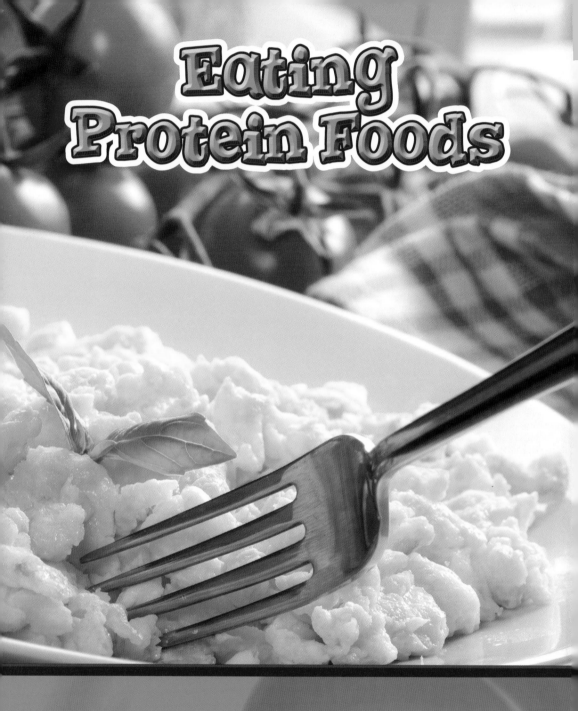

Eggs can be a main dish.
Top scrambled eggs with
cheese for breakfast.

Make an egg salad sandwich
for lunch. Eat a hard-boiled egg
for a snack.

Have fish tacos or beans and rice for dinner.

Try a black bean burger instead of a hamburger. Add vegetables for extra flavor.

19

Nuts taste great in desserts.
Add walnuts to brownies or
sprinkle peanuts over ice cream.

There are many ways to get the protein you need. Try a new protein food today!

Glossary

amino acids—parts of protein foods; amino acids are the building blocks of the human body.

B vitamins—parts of some foods that help your body use energy

fat—a part of some foods that gives you energy and helps your body use vitamins; too much of certain fats is bad for your heart.

iron—a part of some foods that carries oxygen through your blood; this gives you energy.

lean—low in fat

MyPlate—a guide that shows the kinds and amounts of food you should eat each day

omega-3—a fatty part of some foods that is healthy for your heart

poultry—the meat of birds that are raised on farms; chicken and turkey are kinds of poultry.

sodium—salt; too much sodium is bad for your heart and blood.

To Learn More

AT THE LIBRARY

Dilkes, D.H. *Beans, Nuts, and Oils*. Berkeley Heights, N.J.: Enslow Publishers, 2012.

Dilkes, D.H. *Meat and Fish*. Berkeley Heights, N.J.: Enslow Elementary, 2012.

Graimes, Nicola. *Kids' Fun & Healthy Cookbook*. New York, N.Y.: DK, 2007.

ON THE WEB

Learning more about the Protein Foods Group is as easy as 1, 2, 3.

1. Go to www.factsurfer.com.

2. Enter "Protein Foods Group" into the search box.

3. Click the "Surf" button and you will see a list of related Web sites.

With factsurfer.com, finding more information is just a click away.

Index

The images in this book are reproduced through the courtesy of: Tobik, front cover; Stockbyte / Getty Images, p. 4; Juan Martinez, pp. 5, 7, 11, 16, 17, 19, 20; U.S. Department of Agriculture, Center for Nutrition Policy and Promotion, p. 6; RoJo Images, p. 8; Andresr, p. 9; Tom Merton / Getty Images, p. 10; Elena Elisseeva, pp. 12-13; Cappi Thompson, p. 14; Anna Hoychuk, p. 15; Portlandia, p. 18; Jose Luis Pelaez / Glow Images, p. 21.